My Mother's Transvestites

poems by

Tiff Holland

Finishing Line Press
Georgetown, Kentucky

My Mother's Transvestites

POEMS

For Bill and Tori

ACKNOWLEDGMENTS

Some of these poems have appeared in Denver Syntax, Elimae, Slipstream,
Temenos, The Ledge, Mudlark, Exposure, The Cortland Review, Poetry
Midwest, New Zoo Poetry Review, LA Petite Zine, Oklahoma Review,
Atlanta Review, New World Writing, Elm Leaves Journal, Blue Lyra, Fried
Chicken and Coffee.

I'd also like to thank my friends and family for their support as well as the
Hot Pantser, the Kent poets, my friends at USM, Eric Bosse, Andre Dubus
III for his encouragement, Major Ragain, Kathe Davis, Billy Giraldi, and
Virginia Dunn, as well as Inga Wegner and, of course, the anonymous cross-
dresser of Polly Holland's Beauty Salon.

Publisher: Leah Maines
Editor: Christen Kincaid
Cover Art and Design: Joan Wilking
Author Photo: Tiff Holland

Printed in the USA on acid-free paper.
Order online: www.finishinglinepress.com
        also available on amazon.com

Author inquiries and mail orders:
Finishing Line Press
P. O. Box 1626
Georgetown, Kentucky 40324
U. S. A.

Table of Contents

Hot Work

My mother's transvestites like scarves, although none of the women in the shop wear them, not anymore. Slippers-in after closing, they arrive incognito through the back door, emerge sweaty flowers. Being beautiful is hot work but they are willing to pay cash, make concessions, so their wives cannot track their other lives. From high shelves, they try on dusty wigs, dated bouffants, cascading auburn ringlets, sassy shags the beauty-shop ladies spurn.

It is just them and us, my mother and I, dressed for work, she in a smock and me in jeans and Converse, while Jack M., Robert Y., and all the unnamed others, including the vice president of Roadway Trucking, dressed for separate, but equally sparkling galas. Still, they would like nothing more than to mingle under dryers, nibble donuts, discuss *The Enquirer* with the other ladies: mom's Friday, nine-o-clock Joanne; Sandra Hammerstam, Sue Hollinger, and both Big and Little Linda.

My mother applies the transvestites' make-up. I feign sleep in a shampoo chair, sneak peaks at finished products: wingless angels with five o'clock shadow, tottering in circles between the dryers and the styling chairs, trying in that small space to learn to fly.

Foundations

About the time I was trying to decide
whether to have a sex change operation
but before I threw all my dresses and skirts,
my slips and nylons in the trash,
my boyfriend invited me to a fancy nightclub
for New Year's Eve.
The disco ball made me nervous;
I have nothing to wear, I told him,
although I meant:
>I don't know what to wear,
>I don't know who I am.

No problem, he answered.

He drove me to the mall
in his red Ford Escort, took me
to O'Neil's or Kaufman's or Macy's
whatever it was called back then,
found a black velvet bodice with
a crinoline skirt etched in gold.
Part of this is missing, I told him,
though it was lovely.
I couldn't imagine myself in it.
To me it was lovely like
a painting or a flower,
I could no more imagine wearing it
than dressing in petals.

He took me to the foundations department.
I had already told him I was neuter,
had told him on our very first date.
He saw a clerk restocking against the wall.
We need a backless, strapless, black bra,
he announced, his voice floating over the underwires,
his words catching in their cups, he paused.
What's your size? he asked me.
I had never been in that department with someone else.
I only owned athletic bras.

I preferred styles that minimized and
had considered wrapping my chest.
36C, I whispered.
36C, he boomed
and in a moment the thing had appeared.

Vanilla

Still in rollers, cigarette clenched between dentures,
Mom sat at the kitchen table
hands like spades darting back and forth
adjusting the wig.
There, she'd say, and release my wriggling brother,
only to change her mind, bring him back
for another spit pin-curl or to even out his rouge.

Bob was six or seven those summer mornings.
She'd work on him like a mannequin,
fix him up the way she wanted to do with me.
She'd buckle his feet into my abandoned patent leathers,
roll down the tops of bobby sox,
pouf out the party dress,
spin him away and laugh as he twirled.
Last the lipstick; and then,
needing a witness to their mischief,
Mom would send Bob to the neighbor's
and he'd go, for tea and cookies
or maybe just because.

I wouldn't go with him, but I'd watch from the apple tree.
Like Miss America he walked slowly, elegantly,
his head straight, purse clutched to his side.
Sometimes, Mom would dig up an old pair of elbow gloves
that went all the way up Bob's arm, and I'd imagine him
slipping them off to take a cookie,
revealing the dirt under his little boy nails.

The other kids picked on him, called him names,
shoved him in the aisle of the school bus,
and I'd pound them in the street after the bus pulled away.
He was my brother.
But I wouldn't escort him to the neighbor's,
wouldn't nod and agree with my mother:
Isn't Vanilla pretty, isn't your sister pretty?

Once I Wore a Red Bikini

It was our honeymoon,
no one could see me,
no one we knew. We
spent days swimming
in turquoise, napping
in hammocks. I crossed
my legs. My hair was
curly. I was tan; you
were burned.
My thyroid had not
yet eaten my unibrow.
I leaned toward the
camera. Of course,
I thought I was fat
despite the neat crease
at my belly button,
acute angles arranged
to fit inside the frame.

I was happy,
the stroke had not yet
broken my smile.
Earlier, a man
in dreadlocks had
paddled in on a surf
board, right up to
the hotel's buoyed
line, to sell us shells
and a starfish to
place on the mantel,
so that after your
pink skin turned tan,
and years later when
I smelled burnt toast
all the time, every
thing tasting like iron,
we would remember:
once I wore a red bikini.

Flared

My first pair of jeans were flared,
red and white Coca-Cola logo-
swirled, hand-me downs from my
cousin, a boy, my mother reminded,
as if I cared. Before was patent leather,
velveteen jumpers, itchy tights that
took forever to put on, starting at
the vaguely foot-shaped bottom,
alternately pinch-pulling left
and right all the way up to avoid
tears, runners, pulling through
a toe and having to start again.

Occasionally, I wore slacks
with zippers on the side
and no pockets, no place
to jangle loose change, hide
treasures, no access to scratch,
all because I could be pretty
if I would just stand still, cross
my legs; I could be cute with pigtails
a straight scalp line dividing my head
where the hair was pulled apart
and away, bound with elastics
with plastic balls on the ends
leaving me a perky, berried tree.

I was so happy for the mandatory
sneakers of gym class, shorts
in the summer, t-shirts. Winter
was a special hell for girls, shiny
shoes shoved into boots, legs
goose-bumped from ankle to hip,
given mittens and hats, told to keep
warm while covered knee to ankle
with fabric thinner than a condom.

One year for Christmas
I received a muffler, a stuffed animal
to wear, hiding place for my hands
to practice sign language in secret
While my knees pinked with cold,
chapped and bled.

More than anything I wanted overalls,
extra pockets including two long
and thin as pencils, and more denim,
impervious to sharp sticks
and gravel, no doubt the material
bullet-proof vests were made of.

There were no frills, no prettying-
up overalls beyond a red cloth
handkerchief folded into corners
shoved into a chest pocket
or hung from one in the rear.

They had buttons and zippers
and hooks, a loop on one side
for a hammer to be carried
head up, straps that could be
adjusted, raised, or lowered
to leave space at chest level
to cross my arms underneath.

Mom bought my junior-high jeans
at the Acme, the same place
we bought groceries and salt
for the softener. The jeans Mom
called "denims" didn't have
the orange tag on the back pocket
all the kids chased each other around
the playground trying to tear off,
but they were warm and blue, so

fast to put on, shoving a leg in each
hole, then standing, zipping, buttoning,
walking through the door before
the fabric had time to
form itself into creases.

Resemblance

She is tall and thin with my eyebrows,
and everyone says she is beautiful
with her religious curls or iron-
straightened hair; they say she
looks so much like me but I
was never beautiful. Sometimes
Mom said I could be *if*
Only
but I was never beautiful .

She looks just like me.
This is unanimous
in the social media, among
friends and neighbors across
every –olithic era of my life:
that picture of me in a Fozzie
Bear t-shirt eating a chip
at the click of a shutter,
matches one of her
in the backyard, shoulders
wide as mine dangling arms,
each entwined with a BFF.

The serious look from her
Kindergarten graduation?
All me, and there are shots
of me with curls, my chin
cocked the way hers does
when she's *just kidding, Mom.*

She looks like me, yet is
unambiguously beautiful.
So, I wonder: where
is my beautiful?
I never was but sometimes
pretty, which I scorned,
attractive, and striking,

my favorite description,
no doubt to be substituted
for intense, which was
mostly what I was told,
sometimes modified by "too"
by boys
who left in the morning
without clarifying exactly
what they meant.

I was never beautiful, knew
I wasn't beautiful, didn't
want to be or didn't know
I did, until I heard it said
so many times:
your daughter is beautiful.
For years I told myself
I didn't care because
everyone knows
beautiful is for girls.

Elegy for Uncle Bill

In some theories of time,
everything is happening at once,
your birth and death and all your lovemaking:
in one corner of the curved universe,
you're playing catch with your brother
in the backyard, wearing the shorts
and matching ball-caps from the photo
on the shelf beside the kitchen window.

The collie dog from the same picture
is running between you, barking,
and your mitt is new, not yet
shaped to your palm and smelling
of the oil your father is teaching
you to rub into it, as he sits drinking
beer and eating peanuts, listening
to the Indians game.

Or maybe it's 1948, the last year
Cleveland won the Series, and
you know all the players' names,
the batting averages, and ERAs.
You pretend to be Lou Boudreaux
as you run the imaginary baseline
through the tall grass, rounding past
your valedictory speech at second.

There's a throw-down on
the third baseline, and you run
back and forth between your
children and grandchildren before
sliding into home to land
in your backyard with your brother,
the ball curving between you,
spinning in its arc.

No Need for Room Service

Between home and homesick is the highway,
the Day's Inn at Cave City, Kentucky
thirty-seven fifty per night for
king size, bleach-white sheets.
There's a "Triple A" discount and
catfish buffet, "all you can eat."

Just past claustrophobia, we slip
from Central to Eastern Standard Time.
I forget to eat lunch and can't decide
"supper" or "dinner," "sweet corn"
or "greens." I talk to the dog too much.
He lifts his leg at every rest stop in five states.
Knocks us into neutral outside Bowling Green.

I don't know about "true North," but
 I've come to know the South,
barbeque smell on everything,
the shiny-leaved magnolia trees
refusing to curl into fists, fall brown.

"Y'all" is contagious as boiled peanuts
and sweet tea, but I miss that glaze
of frost on the windshield, a
small rectangle scraped
horizontally away.

I like my peanuts roasted, my tea
hot. I like extra blankets, their weight
holding me to my dreams, seasons
so cold they seem clean, devoid
of any other living thing, so that I can't help
but believe in myself, my foggy breath
an echo, my limbs filled with down.

Straightening

Before he put the braces on my teeth
and noting the lithium on my chart
my orthodontist made me promise
never to kill myself, so that the steel
and all his work would not be for naught.
I was wearing the lead-weighted
x-ray gown when he asked
feeling as tied to the earth as I could
being me, being what I am
according to the charts, and
I promised, looking around
to make sure no one else could hear,
not the cheerful hygienists
in their pink coats, or the
woman who made the plaster casts
in her blue coat or the receptionist
in her green lab coat, the whole place
color-coded, and he stuck some
colored stickers on the manila folder
yellow maybe, for coward, or blue
for ....blue..I don't remember, but
I remember wondering
what he expected me to say
if he thought I was a Nostradamus,
that each suicide was born
knowing and waiting
for the braces to come off.

Burning Ghost Money in Akron, Ohio

while
in Taipei, Taiwan the gates
of the hereafter have opened,
allowing the spirits
       out
       to eat,
       sightsee, create
       mischief,
       whisper
to the undead.

Marriages are down, and
real estate sales slow.
Even the doubters offer
       small feasts
to hungry ghosts.
The beaches are less crowded.
       No one
wants to be seen in trunks or
a bikini by deceased
       grandparents.

Here in Akron, Ohio,
my future husband
has
       demanded
my father's ashes
       not
move with me
when our households
       join.

He feels uneasy about
an urn in the living room or
hall. I have stopped
       talking
to my own reflection

in the urn's black
          marble face,
except for
          occasional editorials,

birthday wishes, monologues
          in times of weakness.

Right now, the urn is covered
          in ashy dust
in my half-
          abandoned
apartment.

Anticipating marriage, I
am planning our
          Caribbean honeymoon
from my fiancé's
          bed
for when Ghost Month is over.

Still, before internment,
perhaps a feast.
          Homemade spaghetti
just like I made for him the week
before he died,
          black coffee
and a whole pan
          of fudge.

Carry On

I didn't see your body, didn't think
to ask, picking up a clear baggie
at the nurses' station: watch, wallet,
keys. No clothes, I thought later,
how odd.

At the ATM, you had just enough cash
to pay for your own urn. I bungeed
it to a rolling cart. With a copy of your
death certificate, I brought you home.

Eight years after the divorce, Mom
wondered over your out-of-round
wedding ring. *Where else could it be?*
She said, *he wouldn't give it to Her,*
would he?

Everyone said you were too young,
fifty-two, a good man, the smartest
they ever knew, as they filed in, stood
before pictures pulled from a half-
filled album, squeezed my shoulder,
moved on.

Your suit hovered beside me, drowning
my brother, in his white tennis shoes,
his hands in your pockets, jingling air.

Mom said, *who came up with this music?*
I know what he liked.
All you ever listened to were ball
games, Paul Harvey or elevator music
while you made out contest entries.
I went with "Imagine," "Solsbury Hill."
I know I was projecting, but I was
the one who got on an airplane
alone and flew back with you

in my lap because even dead
you wouldn't fit under the seat
in front of me.

Tracy

can't hold her liquor,
is a flirt but not a tease,
will say anything to anyone,
and has
left me, looking for car keys in bushes,
panties balled at the end of the bed.

Tracy believes
in astrology but not insurance,
likes low-cut blouses
and cheap sentimental jewelry.
Sometimes, she whistles
for no apparent reason, prays
when she thinks I can't hear.

Tracy thinks
recommended daily allowances
are for suckers.
She never gets up
to make sure the stove's off
or check the smoke detector.

Once she went for milk
and came back with a convertible,
traded my Civic for fifty
monthly payments.

My husband asks,
can't Tracy come over
but stops short of please
so he won't seem too eager.
I don't want to know
what they do together.

Tracy plays the wineglasses at parties,
runs a finger over each rim,
adjusts the pitch with sips

of zinfandel or burgundy,
her lips so red, I pale
in comparison,
make her apologies,
try to believe it when I say,
it's not me, it's Tracy.

Tracy at Two AM

Tracy asks a stranger in a bar,
    want a cheap fuck,
gets a chocolate kiss instead.
It's Valentine's Day.
She thinks her heart is broken,
dances so hard she leaves a wake
of vodka, straight.
Tracy tells the man, the boy
who half carries her to her car,
    you look just like my ex-husband
They all look just like her ex-husband.
Only he's not really ex, yet.
Last week he was on dial-a-date,
WKJX-fm, looking for someone
eighteen to thirty-five, someone
who wants a commitment.
It's snowing when she pulls out
onto State Route 43, a snow
as heavy as her eyelids.
She thought she wanted him and now
she thinks she doesn't.
She wants the snow plow to pick her up,
carry her home in its steel embrace.

My Mother's Transvestites

Tracy flirted with them,
with the Jack we called "Jill,"
with the Old Dresser who always
slipped a fifty into mom's cleavage.

Somehow, they found their way
to *Betty Petty's Beauty.*
Perhaps the phone number
was written on the wall
in some gay bar in the Rubber City
or maybe it was word of mouth.

Their appointments were penciled in,
lightly, easy to erase.
After closing, at six or seven
or eight, they'd arrive,
in blue jeans or suits,
driving Lincolns or pick-ups,
just one at a time.

Mom would be washing towels,
emptying ashtrays,
and I'd let them in.
I was her protection,
In case he's a pervert
she always said.

They carried paper sacks
and duffel bags.
They wore glasses
and wedding rings.
They'd push past the beads
between the dryers and the break room,
change in the back.

They'd emerge in strapless,
backless, black evening gowns,

perky cocktail dresses, heels.
None ever wore a duster, or
an apron.

Tracy told them they looked good,
asked them about their days
while mom leaned them
back in the shampoo chairs,
penciled in eyebrows, applied
foundation, blusher, lipstick.

Mom demonstrated when she finished,
do this
the same way she showed me,
and they'd mimic her,
pressing their lips together, carefully,
as if the colors were accidental,
as if they might be permanently stained.

I'd watch them in the three-way,
while I spun circles in the styling chair,
using my tennis shoe toe as brake,
and they'd see me, and not Tracy,
watch my reflection, watch my reflection
look away.

Don't Ask

In my "Gender in Contemporary Poetry" class,
Terry tells us about her pre-enlistment physical,
the Navy gynecologist prodding her
most private parts, violating
the "Don't ask-don't tell" policy, telling
her, as he pins an ovary to her abdominal wall,
she's too cute to be a dyke.

Why are there no love songs for the girl
with an arm like a Yankees short stop,
who hits like Willie Mays?
Why no poems for the girl who makes you
laugh so hard pop spurts out your nose?
I know your first love looked
just like me, blue-jeaned, tennis shoed.
She wore her hair short or under a ballcap,
didn't she? Loved to play practical jokes
and sit with her legs apart.
She could cuss like a sailor, couldn't she,
and whistle through her teeth?
Don't worry, you can admit it;
I won't tell.

Munitions

We used my mother's birth control.
Not the first time, the first time
we didn't think about that,
just about the fumbling
about, what may or may not happen
but other times, later, in her bed
I pushed the spermicidal bullets
out of their silver casings
put them where they could do their work.

The first time was in my old bed
which had been my grandmother's bed
under the light of that window.
Later, the wood rotted,
the whole frame fell out
leaving only the hole,
only the light.

There were many times that year
in the night-dewed grass
of my best friend's yard
in cars, against the garage.
Sometimes we remembered our munitions,
but mostly we didn't,
nothing came of it,
no one.

There was just the one boy,
headed to Basic.
The others couldn't seem to see
what I was underneath the jeans,
the flannel shirts, and high tops,
who I was.

He came back fatigued
with large square pockets,
a tiny black flashlight

we put where the bullets went;
we were amazed at the red glow
my insides themselves still hiding,
the cavity illuminated.

Watch, Necklace, Luggage

When I married and left home at seventeen, Betty gave me three presents: a broken Timex, a necklace with a knot in the chain, and luggage. Actually, Dad gave me the luggage, but he signed "Mom" on the card so, technically, the gift was from her, too. I guess she thought the watch could be fixed, the knot coaxed out of the chain. She said Dad had given her the necklace, and it was a good necklace, platinum with a small diamond. It was the best she had to give me. She had done what she could for the wedding, reserving the Eagles hall for the reception where my Uncle Buddy's band played. Betty requested *Brown Eyed Girl* for obvious reasons and *Mrs. Brown You Have a Lovely Daughter* even though it didn't quite fit. It was close. Donnie's last name was Brown. Betty and my elderly aunts had prepared all the food. My gram paid for the cake. It was a nice wedding for a couple of teenagers, and I was an ingrate for not caring, that's what Betty would have said had I not had the sense to keep my mouth shut. I had wanted to elope, but I went along with it all. Betty insisted on the dollar dance, and good thing she did since the Army screwed up Donnie's pay for the next three months. I couldn't understand why Betty sobbed when I left although I sniffled myself until we got to Canton. Then I stopped.

My Mother's Humility

a found poem

I got my embarrassment
At twelve pole creek
I was messin' with crawdads
Wearing just panties
A group of boys came by
The didn't say anything
Didn't do nothin'
Or even look at me
I had a stick, but
I hadn't been pokin'
But then the boys came
And I knew
By the way I felt
Just the way I felt inside
That I couldn't
Go without a shirt again.

Grandma Gone Out of Breeden West Virginia

At home, the chicken coop
was more sturdy than this house
where the women gathered like hens
around the grandmother in the box,
my mother's gram, laid out
there in the front room, surrounded
by the flowers that grew in the hills.

I turned eight that day and no one remembered.
They were thinking about death,
but I was worried the Cuyahoga-sized crick,
about squatting over the hole
in the outhouse out back.
There might be snakes
like the ones in the funeral service.
The relatives I didn't know swayed
like the snakes they held, and I
blinked and blinked, certain
it was a bad dream, waiting
for the birthday cake that had to come,
trying to keep my balance on the
rope bridge between the crick's banks
knowing it was the only way back.

Purple Town

I grew up between the chemical plant
and the rubber factory, along
a rusty railroad track that ran
out of town in both directions,
named for a matchbox king,
a town with a round lake
and a pair of swans swimming circles
around its endless shores.

The day after the big game,
they painted the streets of my town purple,
and teenage boys marched down them,
bouncing basketballs that rose
just to the tips of their fingers.

The blimp hovered over our heads at night,
its lawnmower motor purring, trailing behind it
the ropes used to tie it down.

I spent the Sundays of my childhood
eating chicken dinners with soggy fries
and hot sauce,
and my adolescence
washing dishes,
making pizzas,
selling collectibles at the local mall.

At seventeen, I moved 500 miles away,
at nineteen, 3000.
At twenty-one, I was back,
ready to embrace my true nature.
I am a chicken eater,
a dish washer,
a blimp watcher.
Everyone I have ever known has worked for companies
named letters of the alphabet:
B&C, PPG, B&W or

for Goodrich, Goodyear, Firestone.
My grandmothers worked in factories,
my father, my grandfather worked in a factory;
my uncles and cousins work in factories
making windows and tires, cars, machines.
For a while, I was foreman
in an automotive transmission ring factory.

My first kiss is the editor
of the local Herald, and I married
my high school sweetheart, and
we all still live in this little purple town.
On the weekends, we go to the Village Inn
pick up mixed dinners, white and dark.
We dunk our fries in the hot sauce,
and we throw away the coleslaw.

In the evenings, we walk around the lake
where the single remaining swan that
refused to take a new mate still swims, or
we drive out to the hanger
watch the blimps take off and land.
They're like big balloons,
men leading them out on ropes
reeling them in on return.
Sometimes when the blimps take off
someone forgets to let go, falls.

Kenny

She always referred to him
as Kenny Rogers, fell for him over
campaign dinners at Republican
Headquarters, *always chicken*, she
said, *always stringy*. She stayed out
later and later, explaining *politics,*
when she returned home smelling
of wine, cigarette smoke and
men's cologne.

She was the campaign
manager
she told us, shoving
hotdogs sliced wide-open
under the broiler, peering
through the oven door
to watch the cheese melt,
Dad's car not yet crunching
down the gravel in the drive
the helium in the redwhiteandblue
balloons already seeping out
above the crepe-papered tables,
her empty chair, waiting.

She freshened her lipstick
compulsively when she talked
about him: his silver beard, his
open shirt, the gold chain across
the hair on his chest,
Just like a BeeGee, she said,
smack, pressing her lips
to a square snatched
from the bathroom roll.

She left tissue kisses
by the phone, on the night-
stand, the passenger seat

of the red Dodge Dart
I dreamt she drove
into Portage Lake, failing
to yield at Cormany,
leaving me to clean up
her affections, perfect
coral lip-prints, the tissues
not wadded or folded
but creased gently
in the middle, then
smoothed flat.

Army Wife

When they finally let me see him, our phone number was written on the blood-splattered sheet. I got the pig farmer next door to drive me to the hospital, since we only had one car, the one he had just totaled. I didn't know it was totaled when I stood beside his bed before they wheeled him into surgery. He was unconscious. There was a jagged cut from his left eyebrow clear to the back of his skull. I was afraid to look too closely. There was a flash of aqua on the exposed bone of the forehead. Later I would find out that was from the other car, a blue Thunderbird. One of them had run the stop sign at the bottom of the hill near the base. Keith's head had gone through the open driver's side window, bounced off the Thunderbird's hood. That's where the blue came from. I was seventeen. I tried to imagine being a widow. I tried to imagine calling his parents and telling them he was dead. Right before the orderly came for him, he woke up. "Don't call the hearse for me, yet," he said. It sounded like horse the way he said it. I didn't call anyone back home. I just waited. The doctor told me he was lucky and gave me a sheet that advised I should wake him every four hours, bring him back if he started vomiting or hallucinating. A cab took us back to our trailer which, for the first time, looked like a long box on its bed of pine needles. His head was wrapped up like a turban. He made me take his picture before he'd go to bed. I shone his Army-issue flashlight into his eyes at twelve and four and eight am. I had never noticed the flecks of brown in his green eyes before, like camouflage, like some mineral trapped in rock.

My Parent's Divorce

After twenty-four years
Wednesdays at seven
sex and spaghetti.

Van Gogh's Ear

Consider the sound of straw rustling,
haystack after haystack
surrounding the countryside
and stars sizzling in the night sky.
Paint has a sound
brushed on a board.
Yellow is the loudest color
it is everywhere.
The inner ear is azure but
first the middle, the tube,
Eustachian,
an entire palette,
sticky, tacky,
too many layers applied
one over another
before the last has dried.
Swallow hard.
Hear that pop?
That's what I was going for—
that clean canvas moment,
perspective falling into place
the angles all right
the silent horizon
just a line, a life,
a space between pigments.

Maneuvers

In the woods, dressed like trees,
we carried weapons green as moss,
painted our faces like jigsaw puzzles,
brown, olive and black stretching
over the topography of faces
underneath our steel-pot heads.
It was important to remember to hold
the compass *away* from our bodies where
our helmets couldn't interfere with True North,
important to know how many of my own footsteps
in one hundred meters, the difference
between a hill and a knoll, how to follow
the glow-in-the-dark eyes taped looking
backwards from the fellow ahead.
There were more deer there at the arsenal
than I had ever imagined.
They ran in herds, ate the growth that grew
above the unexploded rounds buried
there, all around us, some rises
more metal than earth.
We parked the deuce and a half under a tree
in a place a fox had slept so recently
the grass was still hollowed out and warm.
It took me 732 steps to get back,
my finger just off the trigger in the darkness
so I wouldn't have to clean my gun.

Meteorite

I was stretched out in the recliner the night I became a meteorite. I felt it, my body hardening and everything turning into lights, bouncing. I could feel the cavities form from my descent through the atmosphere, and the weave of my shirt stretched tight over my body which had become a field, a field of rocks and cactus and then the ambulance came and they strapped me on for scientific study. My skull was hatched with a latch and inside the rig, they opened it, and I felt myself breaking into pieces, congealing and drifting in the air the way liquids do in outer space, the way since childhood, I had watched astronauts squirt Tang into zero gravity in capsules and shuttles and then open their mouths to drink what looked solid. That's how I felt liquid-solid. I closed my eyes as the plastic mask was held to my open mouth, took a deep breath of space which wasn't black at all, but fluorescent, and tasted like Lucky Charms.

Orange, Brown, Yellow, Red

So creative! Scrawled the art teacher
on the top of my pictures of you
mostly because I used four colors
for your hair, unlike the other kids,
unlike the way I drew other things, although
I branched out to putting lines of blue here and there
in my purely vertical depictions of grass.
She didn't know your hair really was
a mystery, that even though you didn't
own a beauty shop yet, you colored it
over the kitchen sink: blonde, brunette, a
little auburn according to your mood.

The art teacher didn't know that it was
impossible, really, to recreate your hair.
That I didn't have the right crayons,
enough crayons to depict the life of your hair
the way the light hit it revealing red or
orange, how all of this affected the color
of your eyes, which I also mixed, slightly
darker shades, the only steady
the mouse-brown eyebrows you drew
on every morning, sitting in front
of the lighted mirror Dad bought you
for Christmas.

You kept your rollers on the top shelf
in the bathroom, every two or three nights
you'd roll your hair up, hold the waves
in place with the bobby pins you
sometimes used to clean the wax
out of my ears admonishing me
to sit still or you'd slip and I'd end up
deaf.

I liked to play with the porcupine rollers
stacking them like Legos, making

dinosaurs and tube-headed people
I'd pin together, side-by-side
because they were in love. I'd leave
them for you like voodoo dolls, bobby-
pins sticking out at odd angles.

After you'd put your hair up, you'd pull on a
diaphanous blue scarf, skin-cell thin.
I wondered how you could sleep
your head prickly as a cactus, pins
always slipping free, piling
in the corner by the phone where you
smoked and drank coffee while you talked
to your sisters. Others lurked in the sheets,
half-formed curls clinging to them. I'd
take a strand, hold it under the reading light
in the den, try to discern its pigment,
an impossible task.

The Shape of Heaven

I'd like to say it's just a case
 of elevator vertigo,
or maybe it's the heat,
but I'm sleeping in the middle of the day,
and I know all the signs.

We're a fallen race in a fallen world,
and I'm free-falling through the shaft,
can't seem to medicate
the me out of myself.

Once I taught geckos to sing
in a small apartment with mountains
outside the windows.
I had no fear of high places or lizards,
the tails rejuvenating themselves
when met with fate or feet.

The clay was red there, too,
and I played on a softball team
called the Lucky Strikes,
still inventing myself.

Now I'm 998 miles away
from the only home
I've ever known,
still stuck with myself
in a series of rooms.

Heaven is a circular place;
there are no doors, only windows,
and if you fall testing your wings
you grow a tail and try again.

Burgled

I don't tell mom
about the break-in on the phone,
that a stranger took her picture
my wallet, a broken VCR and nine-
inch black and white TV.
I just say *I'm moving.*
I leave out *fast.*

In the meantime, I wedge
a two by four under the knob,
try to peer out of the crack at the jamb.
Nothing is flush any more, or level.

I am the round filling the chamber
in the revolver on the nightstand.
I am the dog's bark, the bolt slid into place.
I am the dial tone, more steady than a heartbeat,
the connection jumping toothpick poles
the length of the country
to ring beside my mother's bed.

A Piece of August

In Ohio, the corn is tasseling,
the dog, practicing homeopathic medicine,
is eating grass again.
Even in my dreams, in which I'm
barren, camouflaged and afraid,
I'm at the mercy of pharmaceuticals.

It's a short season.
The tired flags hang forgotten
from their independence poles
like week-old lynchings.
It is our most incidental qualities
that cause us persecution.

In Mississippi, the love-bugs couple
mid-air only to kamikaze
into oncoming traffic.
Another week and I'll be headed
there again, my second home,
temporarily un-mated, traveling
by means of steel, rubber, asphalt,
unable to remain aloft upon
something as elemental as air.

I never wanted to be Amelia Earhart
or Superman.
I'd rather be Krypto, the superdog
with the power to fly without
Clark Kent's barely disguised
(and constant sense of) responsibility.

I'd be happy just to piss in the tall grass
with the ordinary dogs, oblivious
to our susceptibility, like Superman's
to kryptonite, to be destroyed
by a small piece of our original home.

Vertigo Girl

At forty, my face is too round,
the right side puffy, the left,
numb from an inner-ear imbalance.
My doctor swears the two aren't connected,
but every time the buzzing starts,
so does the tingling.

If my life were a comic book,
if I were a super hero,
I'd be Vertigo Girl,
use my powers of balance distortion
to throw all the crooks off kilter,
leave them sway-legged and silly,
puking like pirates into
the too bright corners of colored panels.

My long-lost cousin says she's had it, too.
Her ENT sent her to a PT who twisted her neck,
sent the tiny stones inside her inner ear
back into place, like marbles
sliding into slots in some children's game.
My ENT prescribes anti-vert, valium,
suggests burrowing into my skull,
inserting a shunt, cauterizing
the too-taut nerve.

When the spinning comes,
I lay very still in my sweat-drenched costume.
The bad guys could come and go, steal
the TV, the computer, the baby, and
all I could do is watch, lock
my eyes on a focal point
will it with my super-vision,
just to stay in one place.

Letter To My Love

Since you left, my
Ziploc bags have lost their seal,
the sound of consonants
makes my teeth ache.

I used to think the sulfur smell after
your showers was proof
of some evil nature, but now
I realize it was just your dandruff shampoo.
I use what's left in the bottle
when I want to feel possessed.

The neighbors have started
to signal each other, my comings
and goings, flicking
their porch lights.
They keep stealing my
one-hundred-watt bulbs.

Even when I'm on the toilet,
the dog checks on me, slouches
in like a teenager, licks
my hand and leaves
eye peeled to the evil tub.

My shrink has started screening
his messages, suggests
I smoke pot.
I know you told
Adam and Trish that I'm
"out of town."

Maybe it's the way
the clouds are bunched up
at the corners, but the
fluorescent sky
seems endless.

I need the answer
to seventeen across.

Kit Car

We made wooden cars from kits and played croquet on the lawn in the park next door to the hospital. It seemed foolish to me, the croquet. We were all heavily medicated, and those mallets are heavy, but we were glad to be out. I remember, the grass seemed so very green after the fluorescent lights of the ward, which turned things just slightly blue and were on all night so the nurses could keep track of us. Outside, we chain-smoked and walked in little circles and lost our balls. None of us knew the rules, not even the aide who checked us out, and after a while, we got tired of the fresh air. We weren't used to it after all, and it seemed odd that no one was watching us, not really, not closely. I mean, we were a danger, each of us, to ourselves or others, and we knew it. So, one by one, we headed for the door; we leaned against the door; we attached ourselves to the side of the building like little Velcro balls on a piece of felt. After a while, it was like we were holding the building up, and we were almost afraid to go inside.

Eulogy for O'Toole

Tomorrow we bury O'Toole
who is nothing to me, not really
and now past tense, too,
related only by marriage,
my mother's second husband;
he's passed on, just past, and
I think about what he'd say about it
ten years ago when it seemed
all his friends were dying
a funeral every week, and he'd go
and talk in a loud voice
about the poor-son-of- a-bitch,
get drunk in the guy's honor.
This was before emphysema and oxygen,
before he burned his house down,
smoking, on his ratty couch,
crying his ex-Navy Seal tears
on the front page of the Beacon Journal
for everyone to see.

The picture today, in the obits is better
but still not good my mom says
a driver's license picture, he looks old.
I don't say that he was old,
that he was old when she married him,
that she knew it; I just agree
to go to the funeral,
remembering a good funeral
second only to St. Patrick's Day
as one of O'Toole's favorite occasions.

As for the two of them,
the wedding day photo tells it all
His arm slung jauntily
over her shoulder, as if
she were just another GI in the jungle,
and her, head up, eyes closed,

looking down her nose in
a floral dress that screams:
This isn't going to work!!
His tie is crooked!
For God's sake she won't allow
ketchup bottles on the table!.
He's looking straight ahead.
He knows this is just another hitch
he has to wait out.

I don't ask her if she's going to
do the funeral home preparations.
She does that part-time
at the very home where he'll be shown.
It seems too strange to imagine her
bent over him, going on the way
I know she would, about his unkempt
nose hairs and wild white eyebrows,
holding his hand in hers one more time
and trimming the nails, talking to him,
gently, the way she did after the fire:
Don't worry 'Toolie;
We're almost done here.

Thanksgiving

The one I always remember is the year
Mom almost cut her finger off
slicing celery for stuffing.
She bled into the turkey and after
the trip to the ER we all
packed up for dinner at Anthe's,
her favorite restaurant and
I always wondered if
that wasn't what she wanted all along,
three-bean salad instead
of creamed corn, hot sourdough
instead of Pillsbury dinner rolls,
real cranberries in a glistening pink glaze
instead of gelled sauce slurped from a can.

I felt like a Pilgrim the year the Indians came.
My uncle sold their turquoise in a kiosk at the mall.
They wore the blue stones
set in silver bracelets and rings.
I was sent to bed without pie
when I asked about the reservation,
the names of the horses they didn't have.

Our last Thanksgiving together,
the year my father died,
he flew in from LA..
I have a picture of us all
pretending we're still a family,
nobody looking at the camera,
or quite looking away.

What the Dead Do

My father orchestrates
the family trips
we never took.
My uncle eats
dry cornflakes
complains my aunt
buys the wrong brand.
My grandmother
calls me *Tiffie*, cooks
what she imagines
to be my favorite foods,
and all my lost dogs
chase invisible balls
across the back pasture
which is dead, too,
burnt to stubble
all the way to the woods.

Spoons

We pierced the apples with sticks, catapulted them at each other. These were the most efficient weapons we could manufacture, better than the bow and arrow sets my brothers received for Christmas, less likely than stones to leave a mark. Summer was a thrum we ran through like a sprinkler, pond-green, a place to wait in the shadows, to king-of-the-hill topple each other, to bring each other down. Our mother just wanted us out of the house. She gave us tablespoons, told us to dig. We emptied a grave of ourselves, filled beach buckets, poured the dirt over our heads until we were dark ghosts. She locked us out of the house but we climbed in the windows, slipped into our sheets. She damned us when she fell into our hole but we were already asleep by then, flat on our backs, still as the dead.

Herr Professor

Herr likes to sprechen Deutsche
in a thick Southern drawl.
He actually believes
in the second person plural,
makes us understand:
y'all's all right.

Herr Professor explains,
Ich bin ein Berliner
while grammatically correct
was a lie either way, Kennedy
neither German nor pastry.
Herr was there, at the Wall,
as close as the snorer in the rear,
stunned, by flung chalk.

Herr rescued, he says, an old map
of the homeland circa 1948.
Tells us: *Next time Germany*
should just buy the extra real estate.

Sometimes, if Schubert's
playing on the radio, he's late
and says we should be, too,
listen a little more to the Masters, to
the magpies, to the magnolia's
pink crescendo as they bloom.

These and Those

These dogs
are not those dogs
one two three
all black and white
running after
Frisbees ball sheep
These dogs sit at my feet
white yellow black
muzzle the hands dangling
at the ends of my arms
They don't watch me sleep

I tested the electric collar
on myself so those dogs
wouldn't chase cars
jumped ten feet at a shock
that didn't faze them
approaching, retreating,
deciding it was worth it,
a singular jolt of pain
to bring order to the universe

These dogs are chaos
bark at their own reflection
in the dishwasher
let us dress them
as Santa Claus
wear bunny ears, they
poke their noses
through the knot-
holes in the fence
to visit neighbor dogs
they recognize as kin, not
another species

Those dogs saw
only the Other even in us

who patted their heads
and brushed their coats
and filled their bowls
It was their job to curtail
our tendencies to wander
to bite to keep us sane.

Fossil

When I ask my toddler why she has torn the lime-green piece of wallpaper from the wall, she explains she is picking flowers. I sprint after her when she lets herself out the sliding glass door wearing only a diaper, my running shoes and a hat. She asks me to pet the pup because she's afraid to do it herself. I stroke his muzzle while she coos *good fella* from a safe distance. When he takes her stuffed hedgehog to his crate for a chew, she screams, *mine, mine, mine* in a voice any species could understand. I realize I am a fossil, just an impression of something that used to be alive. I cry reading The New Yorker in the bathtub. I can hear her in her room, singing, playing the metal faceplate of the heating register like a harp.

Yanked

My lapsed-Amish neighbor is re-siding his house
a little at a time, the way he does everything.
He scrubbed down his garage that way,
leaving six-foot long clean sections to sit for days
before he cleaned the next.
He built his enclosed screen patio from May to July,
a bit at a time, while I watched
from my deck, reading the faithless paper
or daydreaming in the hammock.
He works for an hour,
then rests
and looks at what he's done.
It seems he wills a thing to completion,
sipping iced tea in a folding chair,
staring back at his house,
an audience to his own labor.

He pulled the old siding off a little at a time.
His bungalow was left to stand
in the August Ohio sun
like a hurricane victim,
a plank gone here and there.

Then it was a patched quilt of a house,
equal parts of the old siding and squares
of insulation shining through.
By September, he had it all stripped off.
The house stood for a month,
like a tin foil,
a UFO waiting to take off.

Amish who leave the faith
are said to be "Yanked Over"
to the Yankees.
But my neighbor's ways are nothing like ours.
He does things himself, a little at a time,
watching the ways of God
whether taking a thing down or building it up.

Eclipse Box

Whose birthday is it? she asked.
We were sitting at the kitchen table;
it was covered with orange crayola scribbles.
Nobody's, I answered. I snatched away the crayon;
it broke in two. I stopped and took a breath
and brought out the coloring book. She
started coloring a picture of a bear wearing a hat.
No, whose birthday is it?
She handed me a blue crayon. I felt honored,
she only lets my husband color with brown.
No one's. It's no one's birthday, no one we know.
I thought of Dickinson.
                              I'm nobody who are you?
                              Are you a nobody, too?
Maybe I was missing something. Maybe
on her TV show it was someone's birthday.
Is it Swiper's birthday? I suggested.
NO
There was supposed to be an eclipse.
We had made a box so we could look at it safely.
I thought about birthdays, about cake and frosting,
the way she holds her piece in one hand,
eats from the top down.
Is it my birthday? she asked.
No, not yet. But soon.
I took the box down
from on top of the refrigerator.
I scrunched up one eye, peered
through the hole. Everything
disappeared for a moment,
everything.

Daughter

The girl is slender as the rain. She tells us she's "serious." She talks about her feelings. She likes the rustle of skirts. She makes her own bologna sandwiches, using a cookie cutter to shape them into hearts. She draws pictures of the dog. When we ask why he only has one eye she explains it's because the dog's eyes are not on the front of his face. Looks at us like we're stupid. She draws me with long hair although my hair is short. When I point this out, she draws in scissors so I can cut it. We try to penetrate her brain. We never know when she will cuddle up with her head on a lap or suddenly run away crying. We fear puberty although we have years to wait.

Already Loved

How can I forget the boys,
pinked-up cheeks running
miles around the cinder track,
thin-hair blown back, curled
to their foreheads with sweat?
Or those who used height
to their advantage, flirting
in small spaces and ways,
popping wadded fistfuls
of loose-leaf paper down
and past the opening
of my *top*, my *blouse,*
making way for a goal?

Seventh grade study-hall,
the boy in the row in front
of me, turned his chair around
so we could share a desk, doodle
bi-planes, whole fleets formed
fast. My father had taught me
the tricks, first the fuselage, then
flat ovals of wings as they would
appear, eye-level from the side,
bomb-bay doors penciled
perforations, two small parallel
lines to represent their opening,
the bomb itself depicted in descent,
a twirling choreographed fall.
The secret to our realism: the partial
circles spaced within the propellers'
complete and dotted "O"
keeping the war moving.

I loved first and most the boys I
knew were already loved, whose
mothers dressed them in corduroys
and button-down shirts, who held me

to the almost floral, swirly prints
of their rayon chests during day-time
middle-school dances, despite
my high-tops, my failure
to have taken up the habit of rising
at five to curl hair I kept as short
as theirs, put on a face that wasn't mine.

They smelled so good, grew to be
unrecognizable so quickly, and
completely foreign by middle-age,
while the girls look just the same,
the same face put on and framed
by the same hairstyles until permanent,
only the boys changing, moving
out of their mother's arms, into
blue jeans and t-shirts in college,
studying chemistry and biology,
losing the hair I loved.

I never minded the loved boys'
warm breath in my ear, the inch-
thick lenses that, up close, muddled
my reflection into dark brown
and flesh-colored blobs as abstract
as the patterns of their shirts:
paisley and collared, once so thin
between us. They held me tight
as we danced in place, shifting
our weight from left foot to right,
simultaneously, until we lost
delineation, became a calibrated
blur, so close we could be anything
once we stepped into focus,
anything.

Weathervane

I'm folding myself up a tin-foil hat to wear out in the rain, try to short-circuit this constant buzzing, redirect it with a Kaiserspike, a weathervane made out chicken bone.

I'm candling this ear, this end-of-tonight's broadcasting-static, letting the hot wax cool
into perfect-wicked cochlear images, and then. I'm setting them on fire, burning the sound
down like a lightning-struck tree, a feeble black thread, then I'm giving myself a good yank.

I'm sterilizing needles for acupuncture, studying reflexology. I'm roufa -pounding myself quiet.
All I want is to hear my heart beat, blood pooling into bruises, my own thoughts moving in a straight line.

I'm placing pennies on closed eyelids, drawing all the sounds away from my body theorizing on how it is: bottle trees evict any kind of haint.

Dog bark overwrites exclamation-point script, and there's always the garbage disposal, the dishwasher, to grind to ground, to wash away.

The vacuum cleaner with its attachments designed specifically to exhume dirt and dander, dust and dead cells, is worth a try, but first, the hat, flag-of-surrender folded, shiny side in, or maybe sculpted into a fancy-restaurant left-over swan.

I'm swimming away on a sea of hum-static- hiss-ring-buzz, using it against itself, transmitting to the universe on my private frequency, while I take a bat to my kneecaps, my elbows, my skull.

Every melody deserves harmony. I'm going to inflict time and meter, break the whole notes into quarters, the quarters into eighths. You'll know me when you find me, my shiny hat bobbing, syncopated on a puddle, my craw open like the rooster without the sense to come out of the rain.

The Beauty Shop Ladies

I.

They really want to be movie stars
Elizabeth Taylor, Joan Crawford, Vivien
Leigh. They've seen "The Women",
and they like to lounge on the settee-
shaped shampoo chairs while awaiting
their turn as the focus of my mother's
attention.

They all smoke in the way
of the rich and famous, holding
Salems and Winstons with just
the tips of their middle and fore-
fingers, close to the filters, calling
attention to their manicures,
the hue of their lips.

At the end of the day, the ashtrays
are palette wheels of coral, pink,
and red-tipped butts, sticking
straight up from the ashes like
three-dimensional Pollock paintings,
but during the day, what the ladies
would give for white terry robes.

II.

All week they are wives and mothers.
There are demands and lessons,
dinners to be made or attended.
Here the *girls* bring fresh-this-
morning donuts, coffee
in real china cups raided
from my mother's own cabinet,
and if the lips are chipped, it's
to be expected, overlooked,

the whole place an illusion.

The dryer domes are double-
layered, clear, the inner layer
a planetarium of warm empty,
circular stars converting the
dryer's hum to hot air, the outer
smooth and hard, large, shaped
like a diving bell, an astronaut's
helmet, something that both
delivers oxygen and protects
the head.

III.

It is all about heads. My mother
talks about how many heads
she did today, how many hours
on her feet divided by heads
undifferentiated by shampoo
and set, tint or snip, permanent
wave. I learn time is mutable
flexible, that two events can
occur simultaneously when
more than one woman wants
the coveted Friday morning
nine o'clock appointment.

Then, Mom puts one to work
removing her own curlers
while shaping another's coif,
each content in their own way,
at the attention, Mom talking
to one, rollers removed, curls
falling down, while she pulls
a comb or brush, or even her
fingers through the strands

of the other, straightening,
then shaping.

When she senses feelings of
jealousy arise, she places a
 a rat-tailed comb between
her teeth, feigns concentration
until soon the women, of their
own volition, start to talk
to each other.

IV.

Hair is so undisciplined
but Mom's a master, an
octopus it seems, managing
so many heads at once,
squeezing the tint onto
the grey roots poking up
through the rows of holes
in dye caps, setting the timer,
before she walks away from
and arrives simultaneously,
at her own station, taking up
where she never really left off,
snipping here, and rolling there,
working on seeming Gorgons, careful
not to turn them toward the mirror
until her art is complete, the mythology
contained, lest they all turn to stone.

V.

Each day's count is in the teens,
even Fridays with the loiterers,
the women who arrive before
opening, waiting in their Buicks

and Mavericks, smoking, their
first cigarette of the day in the less
glamourous fashion of solitude,
sucking hard, filling their passenger
compartments with smoke, while
their engines keep running.

The earliest appointments
get first dibs on cream sticks
and fritters, snatch up the as-yet
unwrinkled pages of the weekly
Enquirers. Some have trained
their husbands as chauffeurs,
delight in the absence of car keys
as they enter or exit, leaving
their hands free for one more
pastry for the road, a *borrowed*
publication.

VI.

My brothers and I are most jealous
of all, of her affection and confections,
every night a stale box of leftover
glazed is placed on the kitchen table
in hopes we will ruin our appetites
for the dinner it is too late to cook.
Sometimes, they're so hard
we just lick at icing, other nights
we know nothing else is coming,
and gorge ourselves on their jelly
centers, name them after the Ladies
who have stolen our mother, biting
down on Mrs. Bender, Mrs. Lattimer,
cramming Betty Ratamyer
whole into our mouths.

The Vagina Tax

I admit, when the amniocentesis came back
Girl, I suggested murder-suicide: you, me
the *Girl* in my belly. I refused to birth into
this world another being to make only
seventy-six cents for every dollar
a boy would make. *This,* you said, *is
why your doctor said to continue anti-
depressants through pregnancy.*

At the family reunion I was given two
name tags, one for me, a pledge stuck
to my heart, one affixed firmly, navel-
level to my shirt stretched red, with
thin white stripes. In pictures, it looks
like an EKG. The girl kicked hard after
sweets, while I swam in the lake. I
consoled myself with the thought
of us swimming in tandem mother
within Mother.

Once she was out, she rode your belly
to sleep, curved to your form, instead
of yours curving to hers. She woke me
every three hours. I wrote R on one side
of an index card, L on the other, so I
could keep track of my sanguination,
thumbed through channels, trying
to stay awake.

Your daughter, my step-daughter
calls you *He, Him*, says she needed
years of therapy because of *That Man.*
I tried to imagine why, as you cut
our ten-year old's pizza into bite-
size pieces, put whipped cream
on waffles, root beer, the tip
of her nose.

Now, I have to take her with me, to
my mother's funeral, to another state,
to places you haven't conceived
of, and you won't understand, the
way you dismissed the vagina tax.
You will always want to shape the both
of us to your form, imagining yourself
Atlas, holding us up, not knowing
your hands stand in the way of our
necessary revolution.

The Last Dress

The last dress was black, silk,
sleeveless. It had no pockets,
no pattern or texture, no frills.
It may have had a name or type
A-line, sundress, column or
mermaid. All I know for certain
is it wasn't a ball-gown; it held me
close and straight.

By the time I last wore it,
I had requirements:
wedding or funeral, over
seventy degrees, my
attendance obligatory,
the costume, for that is
what is was by then,
donned only for a relation
or true friend.

I wore a strand of pearls,
dangly earrings, stockings
and a slip. My shoes had no
heels. Someone
took a picture in which
I am half a handsome couple
uncertain what to do
with my hands.

It was the most harmless
of my dresses. It could
have been halved, hemmed
to a sleeveless shirt, something
I could wear every day without
feeling I was betraying myself.

I held onto it after the initial
purge which was fueled

by ambivalence and practicality.
I left it just-in-case hanging
while I dragged green plastic
garbage bags trailing nylons,
bursting with hangers, to the curb.

When my apartment was burgled
all my jewelry, understated
as it was, stolen, I stopped
wearing any, felt more and more
like all adornment was drag,
the draft under a dress a threat
of opportunity, I couldn't risk.

In my closet, the silk held dust
like a skein, dry-clean only.
I couldn't brush it off or
wash it out. I was just beginning
to recognize who I really am,
to bristle under the preposterous
necessity of crossing my legs simply
because I belong to that portion
of the population who *should*.

Someone told me,
It's all about the accessories.
I said I stopped wearing the dress
because I had nothing to wear
with it, no shoes, no earrings.
Really, I abandoned it because
I had no where to go in which
I had any reason to be someone
other than myself.

Tiff Holland's poetry and prose appear regularly in journals and anthologies including: *New World Writing, Elm Leaves Journal, New Flash Fiction* and many others. Her chapbook *Bone in a Tin Funnel* is available from Pudding House Press. Tiff is the author of the award-winning flash fiction chapbook *Betty Superman* from Rose Metal Press which later adapted the collection as a novella-in-flash and featured it in the collection *My Very End of the Universe* which won an IPPY award. Born and raised in northeast Ohio, Tiff has lived, worked, and studied in Georgia, Mississippi, Hawaii, and Texas. She earned a BA in Philosophy from Kent State as well as an MA in Literature. She received her PhD in Creative Writing from The Center for Writers at the University of Southern Mississippi.

www.ingramcontent.com/pod-product-compliance
Lightning Source LLC
Chambersburg PA
CBHW021158090426
42740CB00008B/1144